THE GEOMETER'S SKETCHPAD®

Learning Guide

Key Curriculum Press
Key College Publishing

The Geometer's Sketchpad®

Dynamic Geometry® Software for Exploring Mathematics
Version 4.0, Fall 2001

Sketchpad Design: Nicholas Jackiw

Software Implementation: Nicholas Jackiw and Scott Steketee

Support: Keith Dean, Jill Binker, Matt Litwin

Learning Guide Author: Steven Chanan

Production: Jill Binker, Deborah Cogan, Diana Jean Parks, Caroline Ayres

The Geometer's Sketchpad project began as a collaboration between the Visual Geometry Project at Swarthmore College and Key Curriculum Press. The Visual Geometry Project was directed by Drs. Eugene Klotz and Doris Schattschneider. Portions of this material are based upon work supported by the National Science Foundation under awards to KCP Technologies, Inc. Any opinions, findings, and conclusions or recommendations expressed in this publication are those of the authors and do not necessarily reflect the views of the National Science Foundation.

Key Curriculum Press
1150 65th Street
Emeryville, CA 94608 USA

http://www.keypress.com/sketchpad
techsupport@keypress.com

Printed in the United States of America
10 9 8   08 07 06
ISBN 1-55953-530-X

Contents

The Geometer's Sketchpad Learning Guide

Introduction

Welcome to The Geometer's Sketchpad! Whether you are new to Sketchpad or an experienced user, this Guide is designed to help you learn about this dynamic math visualization tool in a practical, fun way.

What Is The Geometer's Sketchpad?

If you have yet to install the program, you may want to skip ahead to Installing Sketchpad (page 7) and do that now.

For millennia, *drawing* and *visualization* have been important parts of mathematics. A primary skill taught in geometry classes has long been compass and straightedge construction; in algebra, it's been function plotting. Paper-and-pencil work will always have an important place in math classrooms, but it has two major drawbacks: It's time-consuming (or sloppy), and the finished products

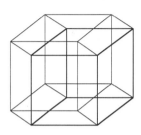

A "hypercube" (4-dimensional cube) created in Sketchpad

are static. It's easy to see how a computer program like The Geometer's Sketchpad can solve the time problem: Commands such as **Angle Bisector** and **Reflect** instantly perform tasks that would take a much longer time with pencil and paper, allowing you to construct and explore many more—and much more complex—figures in a given amount of time.

Dynamic Mathematics

To truly understand the power of Sketchpad, however, you have to understand the second "problem"—that paper-and-pencil constructions and plots are *static* (as are figures in books, blackboard drawings, and most graphing calculator plots). Some things that may

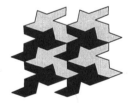

seem true about a construction (that certain angles are congruent, perhaps) are in fact mathematically true. But other things may just *appear* to be true due to *choices* made during the construction. It's very difficult to distinguish what's *sometimes* true from what's *always* true without going back and doing more constructions. Similarly, it's difficult to draw conclusions about a family of curves, such as $y = mx + b$, without plotting many such curves.

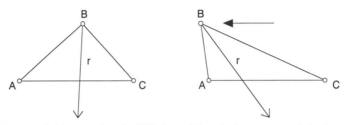

Ray *r* is an angle bisector of angle *ABC*. Some things that may appear to be true in the figure on the left, such as the angle bisector possibly bisecting the opposite side, are easily seen to be not true once point *B* is dragged.

The real beauty of constructions made in Sketchpad is that they are *dynamic*. Sketchpad constructions can always be dragged, squeezed, stretched, or otherwise changed while keeping all mathematical properties intact. As a figure is manipulated, relationships defined by the construction (that one segment is perpendicular to another, for example) continue to hold, and the only properties that change are those not strictly determined by the construction. So, by manipulating a Sketchpad figure, you can explore many of the possible forms it can take given a certain set of conditions. This makes it easy to distinguish between properties that are *sometimes* true and those that are *always* true. Similarly, by animating parameters *m* and *b* in *y = mx + b*, for example, you can explore an entire family of curves in just one sketch.

What Can You Do with Sketchpad?

In addition to using it in his teaching and tutoring, the author of this Guide has used Sketchpad to design quilting patterns for a friend and to arrange furniture in his living room!

The Geometer's Sketchpad is an amazingly flexible tool, so the possibilities for how you can use it are limited only by your imagination. Here's a small sampling of things you can do with Sketchpad.

Explore and Teach Theorems from Geometry

Geometry textbooks are filled with definitions, postulates, theorems, corollaries, and lemmas. Many of these are hard to understand, and even when understood, don't always sink in easily. A great way to figure out these tough theorems—or to teach them in class—is to model them in Sketchpad. (An example of this can be seen in Tour 2: A Theorem about Quadrilaterals.)

Make Classroom Presentations

A *presentation sketch* is a Sketchpad document designed for presentation (or distribution) to a group of people, such as your students, classmates, or teacher. Presentation sketches usually have striking graphics and often involve animation, action buttons, and several pages of content. Teachers can use Sketchpad as an effective teaching tool—even if they don't have daily access to a computer lab—by showing and working with presentation sketches on a single classroom computer hooked up to an overhead projector. Students can also use presentation sketches to make classroom presentations or to create reports or portfolios.

Study Figures from a Textbook

When you become proficient using Sketchpad, you'll find that it can take less time to construct a figure on the computer than it does to copy it accurately by hand. Besides, once the figure is constructed in Sketchpad, you gain the advantage of having a dynamic figure to

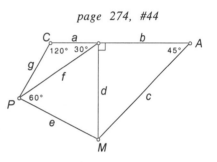

page 274, #44

manipulate and explore. So, consider using Sketchpad to construct and study textbook figures for your nightly homework (or for classroom discussion the next day if you're a teacher).

Use Sketchpad in All Your Math Courses

Several books about using Sketchpad in different math subject areas are available from Key Curriculum Press, and many other resources are available online. The Sketchpad Resource Center at www.keypress.com can point you toward many such resources.

You'll find that Sketchpad is an indispensable tool for all your math courses, whether you're a student or a teacher. In algebra, you can use Sketchpad to investigate slopes and equations of lines, properties of parabolas, and many other important topics (see Tour 7: Algebra Potpourri). Advanced algebra and pre-calculus students and teachers can investigate dynamic families of functions using features from the Graph menu. Use Sketchpad in trigonometry courses to investigate the connections between right triangles and the trigonometric functions. Calculus students and teachers can investigate derivatives using sketches

of tangents to functions and the **Derivative** command; or they can explore integrals using sketches of areas under curves. College mathematics majors will continue to find Sketchpad useful as they study non-Euclidean geometry and other advanced mathematics topics.

Construct Fractals

Check out Tour 8: Constructing a Snowflake to see just how easy it is to construct a striking fractal image: the Koch Snowflake.

Fractals are striking geometric forms that are found in nature and that serve as the basis of many computer graphics programs. A fractal is a geometric figure that is *self-similar:* It looks the same at any viewing magnification. Constructing a fractal involves making a simple construction, then applying that construction to smaller and smaller parts of the figure. Sketchpad's **Iterate** command makes this type of construction possible, as well as other types of constructions that involve repeated processes.

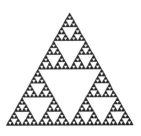

Create Perspective Drawings and Other Geometric Art

Want to create a unique greeting card or a funky background design for your web page? With Sketchpad's transformational tools, combined with features from the Display menu and elsewhere, you can create some amazing artistic images.

About This Book

There's nothing preventing you from doing all eight tours at once, or in a few sittings, but it probably would help to spend some time exploring on your own between tours.

The guided tours in this book provide a step-by-step introduction to all of Sketchpad's major features and many advanced applications. If you're a newcomer to Sketchpad, you should start at Tour 1 and work your way through at least the first four tours for starters. If you're an experienced user, you should glance through the early tours with an eye out for a helpful tip here or there. When you reach a point where most of the information is new, follow along from there.

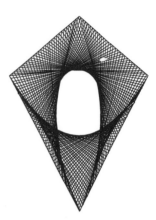

Guided Tours

Here's an overview of the eight tours:

Tours 1–4 form a group called An Introduction to Sketchpad. These tours serve as a basic introduction to Sketchpad, each focusing in some way on quadrilaterals.

Tour 1: Constructing a Square
Here you will construct your first Sketchpad figure: a square. You'll learn how to use the **Segment** and **Compass** tools, as well as the **Intersection**, **Parallel Line**, and **Perpendicular Line** commands. You'll also learn how to test your constructions using the "drag test."

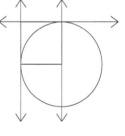

Tour 2: A Theorem about Quadrilaterals
You'll construct a simple figure (using some new commands from the Construct and Measure menus) and use it to investigate a theorem from geometry. You'll see how dynamic geometry enables you to generalize about a whole class of figures from a single construction. You'll also learn how to create captions for your sketch using the **Text** tool.

Tour 3: String Art
Using the **Trace** command and both the **Animation** command and an Animation action button, you'll create beautiful "string art" in Sketchpad.

Tour 4: A Bestiary of Quadrilaterals

This tour introduces multi-page documents with a pre-made collection of quadrilaterals. You'll learn to navigate the pages of this document, explore a construction using its Object Properties panel, and turn an existing construction into a custom tool that can be used to repeat the construction automatically.

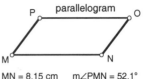

MN = 8.15 cm	m∠PMN = 52.1°
NO = 4.25 cm	m∠MNO = 127.9°
OP = 8.15 cm	m∠NOP = 52.1°
PM = 4.25 cm	m∠OPM = 127.9°

Tour 5: Reflection + Reflection = ?

Tours 5–6 form a pair called Transformations.

What transformation results from the composition of two reflections? As you explore this question from transformational geometry, you'll be introduced to several commands from the Transform menu, as well as Sketchpad's Calculator.

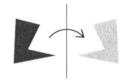

Reflection

Tour 6: Building a Kaleidoscope

Building upon the figure from Tour 5, you'll define your own custom transformation tool, then use it to further explore transformations and symmetry in Sketchpad. You'll then use animation and the **Merge** command to create a beautiful, yet simple, kaleidoscope.

Tour 7: Algebra Potpourri

One tour is hardly enough to cover the possibilities for algebra with Sketchpad, so this tour gives you a taste of several different applications, including function plotting, plotting a family of curves using parameters, and exploring a function involving circles.

Tour 8: Constructing a Snowflake—Iteration

Here you'll use the **Iterate** command to construct a fractal called the Koch curve. You'll turn your construction into a custom tool and use that tool to make a Koch Snowflake.

Installing Sketchpad

The following two sections describe how to install The Geometer's Sketchpad for Windows® and Macintosh®, respectively.

Windows Installation

Insert the CD in your CD-ROM drive and follow the instructions on the screen. If the setup program does not run automatically, follow these steps:

1. Display the files on the Sketchpad CD.

2. Run the program named "Setup Sketchpad.exe."

3. Follow the onscreen instructions.

Macintosh Installation

1. Insert the CD in your CD-ROM drive.

2. Double-click the icon labeled "Install."

3. Follow the onscreen instructions.

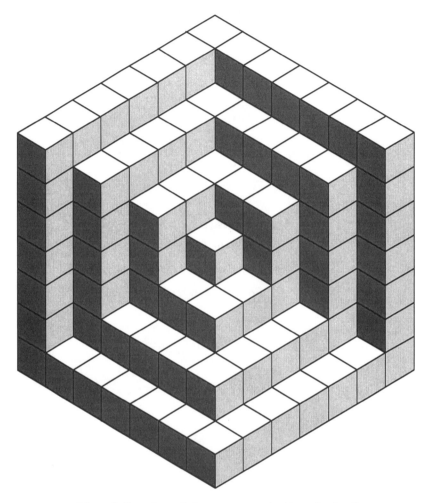

A tessellation of parallelograms, or a stacking of cubes?

The Basics

This section describes the fundamental computer skills you will need to use Sketchpad and the basics of Sketchpad itself. If you are relatively new to Windows or Macintosh, read this entire chapter. Otherwise, browse the chapter, focusing on the Toolbox section and later, or just skip ahead to the Tours.

What You Should Know about Your Computer

If you are entirely new to Windows or Macintosh, start by reading the manuals that came with your computer. Be sure that you are familiar with the following terms describing mouse activities:

Point   Move the mouse until the tip of the current tool is over the desired object.

Click   Press and release the mouse button quickly. (Use the left mouse button in Windows unless instructed otherwise.)

Double-click   Click the mouse button twice in rapid succession. (Use the left mouse button in Windows.)

Drag   Point at the object you wish to drag, then press and hold down the mouse button (the left mouse button in Windows). Move the mouse to drag the object, then release the mouse button.

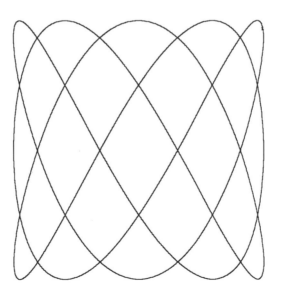

What You Should Know about Sketchpad

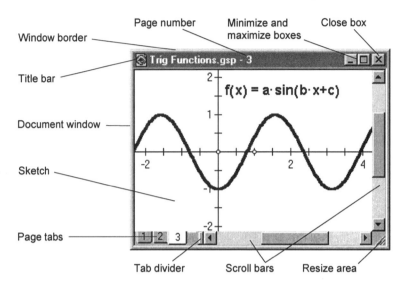

Document Window (Windows)

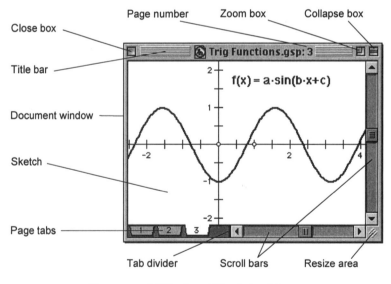

Document Window (Macintosh)

The Geometer's Sketchpad Learning Guide

The figures on the previous page show the document window as seen on typical Windows and Macintosh computers. The following controls are common to both platforms:

Title bar:	Drag to reposition the window on the screen.
Close box:	Click to close the window.
Page tabs:	Click to change pages (only present if your document has more than one page).
Tab divider:	Drag to provide more or less space for page tabs (only present if your document has more than one page).
Scroll bars:	Click or drag to scroll the window.
Resize area:	Drag to change the window's size.

Because some sketch objects, like lines and rays, extend beyond the normal scrollable area, you can always press a scroll bar's buttons even when the scroll bar itself is at its limit.

Several of the controls depend on which type of computer you have. If you're using a Windows computer:

Window border:	Drag any border of the window to change its size.
Maximize box:	Click to expand the window to the largest possible size.
Minimize box:	Click to shrink the window to an icon.

If you're using a Macintosh computer:

Zoom box:	Click to expand or contract the window.
Collapse box:	Click to shrink the window to its title bar only.

Using Menus

Choosing a Command from a Menu

(Note: The graphics for these steps are on the top of the next page.)

1. Point the cursor at the name of the menu containing the command you wish to use.

2. Click on the menu name. (On some computers, you may need to press and hold down the mouse button.)

   The menu drops down to display the commands. Each command is highlighted as you move the cursor over it. If a command is dimmed, it's not currently available.

3. Move the pointer down the menu until what you want is highlighted, then click (or release) the mouse button.

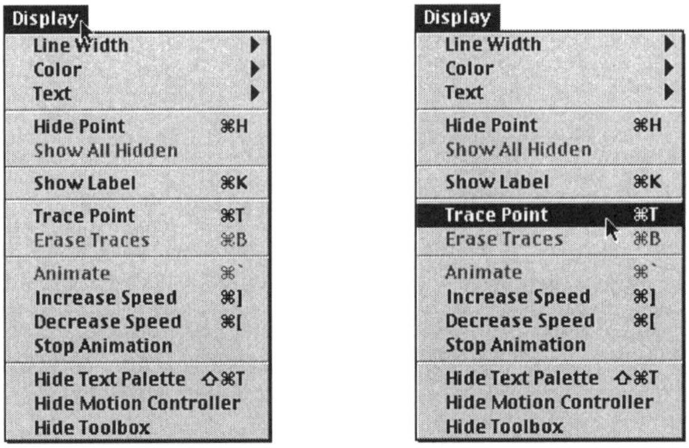

Choosing a command from the Display menu (Mac)

Why Are Some Menu Commands Dimmed?

When you look at a menu (such as the one above), you may notice that some commands appear in dim, gray text (**Show All Hidden**, **Erase Traces**, and **Animate** above). These commands are not available at the moment because they require some special condition to be met. For example, **Show All Hidden** is only available if you've previously hidden at least one object in the active sketch. This Guide will explain when commands are available and why.

Choosing Menu Commands with Keystrokes

In the menu shown above, the **Trace Point** command has a symbol to the right of it: ⌘T (Ctrl+T on a Windows machine). This indicates an alternate way to access the command other than choosing it from the menu: a keyboard shortcut. On a Windows machine, hold down the Ctrl key and press T to access this command from the keyboard. On a Macintosh, hold down the ⌘ key (the "command" key) and press T.

Choosing a Command from a Submenu

Note in the Display menu above that the first several commands have triangles next to their names. This means that each of these commands has a submenu of choices. To choose a command from a submenu:

1. Display the menu and move the cursor to the command you want.

   The submenu appears.

2. Move the cursor over the triangle and down the submenu to the command you want.

3. Click (or release) the mouse button.

Choosing an item from a submenu (Windows)

Dialog Boxes

Menu commands ending in an ellipsis (…) will bring up a dialog box asking for additional information.

Dialog boxes allow you to supply additional information required by some commands. For example, when you choose the **Translate** command from the Transform menu, the dialog box to the right appears. When you have chosen the desired options and entered the proper information, click Translate to proceed. Click Cancel if you decide you don't want to perform the command at all. Click on the question mark (Mac) or Help button (Windows) to bring up online reference material on the current dialog box. (In Windows, you can also press the F1 key.)

Translate dialog box (Mac OS X)

The Toolbox

The Toolbox (initially located along the left side of the sketch window) contains tools for selecting, dragging, creating, and labeling objects, as well as for accessing custom tools.

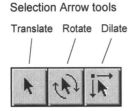

Selection Arrow tools	Selects and drags objects. There are actually three **Selection Arrow** tools (see Choosing a Tool from a Palette, below). The individual tools translate, rotate, and dilate objects, respectively.
Point tool	Creates points.
Compass tool	Creates circles.
Straightedge tools	Creates segments, rays, and lines. There are three **Straightedge** tools, one for each type of straight object.
Text tool	Creates and manipulates labels and creates caption boxes.
Custom Tools menu	Contains a list of available custom tools and commands for creating and working with custom tools.

Choosing a Tool from the Toolbox

Click on the tool you wish to use. The tool remains active until you choose another tool.

Choosing a Tool from a Palette

The **Selection Arrow** tools and the **Straightedge** tools are actually palettes of tools.

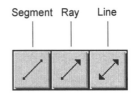

To choose a tool from either of these palettes:

1. Position the cursor over the current **Selection Arrow** tool or **Straightedge** tool in the Toolbox.

2. Hold down the mouse button to display the entire palette.

3. Drag to the right until the tool you wish to use is highlighted, then release the mouse button.

Tours 1–4: An Introduction to Sketchpad

In this series of tours focusing on quadrilaterals, you'll learn many of Sketchpad's fundamental features. You'll construct, manipulate, and examine quadrilaterals, create artwork based on quadrilaterals, and explore a theorem from geometry about quadrilaterals. When you've completed all four tours—in addition to perhaps being a bit tired of quadrilaterals!—you'll be an adept Sketchpad user with a good understanding of the software's basic operations.

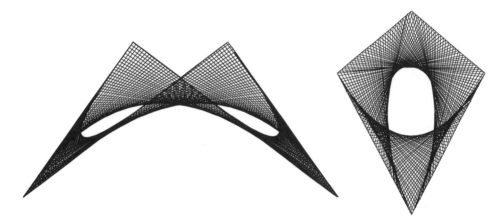

Along the way, feel free to experiment as much as you want. By trying things out on your own, you'll learn in the way that's best suited to *you*. Besides, one of Sketchpad's best features is its *unlimited undo*. This means that by repeatedly choosing **Undo** from the Edit menu (or pressing Ctrl+Z on Windows or ⌘+Z on Mac), you can backtrack as many steps as you'd like, all the way back to the beginning of your current session! So . . . Experiment. Fiddle. Play. You can always get back to where you were and rejoin the tour from there.

Tour 1: Constructing a Square

In this tour, you'll play around with Sketchpad's basic tools and get a first taste of constructing a geometric figure—a square.

What You Will Learn

- How to use the **Undo** command to backtrack through your actions.

- How to construct segments and circles.

- How to select and drag objects.

- How to construct lines that are perpendicular or parallel to other lines.

- How to construct points at the intersection of two objects.

- How to save Sketchpad documents.

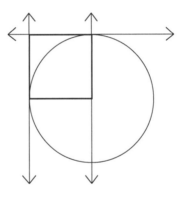

Free Play

If this is your first experience with Sketchpad, you may find it hard to resist playing with the tools and menu commands. We'll start this tour by encouraging you to do just that, giving you just a little guidance.

1. Start Sketchpad if it isn't already running or choose **New Sketch** from the File menu.

   A new, blank sketch window appears.

GSP 4.0

The Geometer's Sketchpad Learning Guide

2. Try each of the following:

You'll learn more about each of these tools throughout the tours.

- The **Point, Compass,** and **Segment** tools (shown top to bottom at right as they appear in the Toolbox) are known as the *freehand* tools. Use these tools to draw objects in the sketch plane (the main part of the window). Click on a tool in the Toolbox to choose it. Then click in the sketch to construct objects. Click once with the **Point** tool to draw a point. Click twice (in different locations) with the **Compass** and **Segment** tools to draw circles and segments. Try clicking in different places—sometimes in blank space and other times on objects you've already constructed (points, circles, and segments).

- Once your sketch is "well-populated," choose the **Selection Arrow** tool from the Toolbox. This tool is used for selecting and dragging objects. Practice dragging; in particular, drag objects that are attached to other objects. To deselect all objects, click in blank space.

- Click on objects with the **Text** tool to show or hide labels. Double-click objects or labels to change a label. Double-click (or press-drag-release) in blank space to start typing a caption.

- Using the **Arrow** tool again, select one or a small number of objects. See what commands are available in the menus and try some out. You'll find that some commands are available for most types of selections, whereas others require specific selections in order to be available.

Getting Serious

3. When you're ready to move on, do the following: Choose **Undo** from the Edit menu—or better yet press Ctrl+Z on Windows or ⌘+Z on Mac—to backtrack through your work.

   *Note: Holding down either keyboard combination causes Sketchpad to undo repeatedly. Hold down the Shift key while choosing **Undo** to **Undo All** in one step. To redo undone steps, choose **Redo** from the Edit menu (Ctrl+R on Windows or ⌘+R on Mac).*

If the **Straightedge** tool looks different from the one pictured, press and hold the mouse button over the current **Straightedge** tool and choose the **Segment** tool from the palette that appears.

4. You should now be working in a blank sketch. Choose the **Segment** tool from the Toolbox.

5. Construct a horizontal segment to be the bottom side of your square. Hold down the Shift key while doing this to help keep the segment horizontal.

After step 5

6. Choose the **Compass** tool from the Toolbox.

   Why do you think you'll need a compass—a device for drawing circles—in order to construct a square?

7. Position the **Compass** tool over the right endpoint of the segment.

   The point is highlighted, indicating that it will be the center of the circle you're about to construct.

Note: If you get stuck at any point in this tour, just open **Tour1_StepByStep.gsp** in the **Tours** folder (which is inside the **Samples** folder next to the application itself). There are StepByStep sketches for most tours.

8. With the right endpoint highlighted, click the mouse button. Move the **Compass** tool toward the other endpoint (you'll see the circle you're constructing as you drag the mouse). Click a second time when the left endpoint is highlighted.

   A circle is constructed, centered at the right endpoint and passing through the left endpoint.

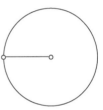

After step 8

Remember: The **Arrow** tool is used for selecting and dragging objects.

9. Using the **Selection Arrow** tool, drag each of the two points in the sketch to be certain that the circle is attached to the segment. If it's not, and there are actually more than two points in the sketch, choose **Undo** from the Edit menu until the circle disappears. Repeat steps 6–8, taking care that the **Compass** tool is positioned over the right endpoint first and over the left endpoint second. (Each endpoint should be highlighted when clicking.)

10. Click with the **Arrow** in blank space to deselect all objects.

    It's important to deselect objects (by clicking in blank space) before making new selections. Otherwise, you may end up selecting more objects than you intended.

Constructing Perpendicular and Parallel Lines

Next you'll construct a line through the center of the circle and perpendicular to the segment. Notice that we had to state both things—"through the center of the circle" and "perpendicular to the segment"—to be clear which line we meant. Similarly, Sketchpad needs two items selected—a point and a straight object—to construct a perpendicular (or parallel) line.

11. Select the segment and its right endpoint by clicking on them with the **Arrow**. Choose **Perpendicular Line** from the Construct menu.

    A line is constructed through the selected point perpendicular to the selected segment.

12. With the line still selected, select the circle as well. Then choose **Intersections** from the Construct menu.

    Points appear where the line and circle intersect.

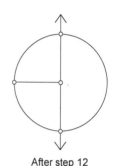

After step 12

To construct a parallel line, Sketchpad needs to be given a straight object to be parallel to and a point to pass through (just as with perpendicular lines).

13. Deselect all objects by clicking in blank space. Select the topmost point just created and the original segment. Then choose **Parallel Line** from the Construct menu.

    Another line is constructed.

14. Use either **Perpendicular Line** or **Parallel Line** to construct a vertical line through the left endpoint of the original segment.

    Use the same technique you used in step 11 or step 13.

15. Deselect all objects. Select the two lines from the last two steps and choose **Intersection** from the Construct menu.

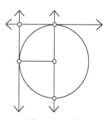

After step 15

Completing the Construction and Doing the "Drag Test"

There are many reasons for dragging; exploring related cases, comparing measurements, and creating visual patterns are a few. But when the purpose is to test whether a construction "holds together," we call that the *drag test*.

There's still a little "polishing" to be done, but you now have the four points defining your square. Take a moment to drag various parts of the sketch around. As an object is dragged, Sketchpad moves related objects to preserve the mathematical relationships used to define the figure. For example, no matter how things are dragged, the line you constructed through the center of the circle is always perpendicular to the original segment. Why? Because that's how you defined it in step 11!

16. Select everything *except* the four corners of the square and the original segment. You'll know that you've selected the right number of objects if the *Status Line* says "Selected: 5 Objects."

    The Status Line is the informational text that appears in the bottom right (Mac) or bottom left (Windows) corner of the sketch window.

17. Choose **Hide Objects** from the Display menu.

    You should see only the four corners and bottom side of the square. If you hid the wrong objects, just choose **Undo Hide Objects** *from the Edit menu and try again.*

After step 17

18. Using the **Segment** tool, construct the remaining three sides of the square.

Voilà! You have now made your first Sketchpad construction!

Is your figure a square no matter how you drag its parts? If not, it's not a true Sketchpad square. This is the essence of the "drag test."

19. Use the **Selection Arrow** tool to once again drag different parts of your square.

20. Choose **Save** from the File menu. Give your sketch a descriptive name, such as `Square`, and click Save.

    Remember where you saved this sketch because you'll need it in a later tour.

Further Challenge

Before going on, you may want to try some constructions on your own. Using the techniques you've learned so far, try constructing a parallelogram, a rectangle, or a rhombus. Don't forget to test your constructions using the drag test. Don't worry if you can't figure all of these out—the techniques covered in the upcoming chapters will build on what you've learned here.

The Geometer's Sketchpad Learning Guide

Tour 2: A Theorem about Quadrilaterals

Sometimes in math, you'll run across a theorem that doesn't make a lot of sense, doesn't jibe with your intuition, or just doesn't make enough of an impression to stick in your brain. A great way to deal with this type of situation is to explore the theorem in Sketchpad. In this tour, we'll present a geometry theorem in the form of a challenge. As you solve the challenge, you'll learn many new Sketchpad features.

What You Will Learn

- How to construct a polygon using the **Segment** tool.

- How to show an object's label.

- How to measure lengths and angles.

- How to create a caption.

- How to apply formatting options to text.

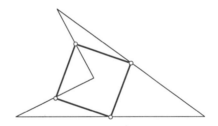

When the midpoints of the sides of a quadrilateral are connected, the resulting shape is always a _____.

This theorem from geometry has a key word left blank. Our goal is to use Sketchpad to discover what word fills the blank. Don't worry if this theorem seems a bit beyond you now or, on the other hand, if it's too simple. The point is to learn about how to use Sketchpad for making and testing conjectures.

Constructing a General Quadrilateral

A "general quadrilateral" is a quadrilateral with no special properties, such as congruent sides or right angles.

1. Start Sketchpad if it isn't already running. If it is running, choose **New Sketch** from the File menu.

2. Use the **Segment** tool to draw a segment.

3. Construct a second segment that shares one endpoint with the first.

    The shared endpoint will highlight before you click on it if the tool is in the proper spot.

After step 3

4. Construct two more segments to complete the quadrilateral.

5. Using the **Arrow** tool, drag some of the points and segments to make sure the figure holds together.

    This is once again the "drag test." If your quadrilateral doesn't stick together, undo several steps and draw new segments, taking care to connect the endpoints.

After step 5

Constructing the Inscribed Quadrilateral

Now that you have a quadrilateral, recall the theorem you're exploring. It starts out: "When the *midpoints* of the sides of a quadrilateral are *connected . . .*" You will continue by constructing the four midpoints and then connecting them.

6. Deselect all objects by clicking in blank space. Select the four sides of the quadrilateral in clockwise or counterclockwise order.

Since four segments were selected, all four midpoints will be constructed at once.

7. Choose **Midpoints** from the Construct menu.

8. With the four midpoints still selected, choose **Show Labels** from the Display menu.

9. With the four midpoints still selected, choose **Segments** from the Construct menu.

    The inscribed quadrilateral is constructed.

After step 9

The Geometer's Sketchpad Learning Guide

Dragging and Measuring to Confirm Your Conjecture

Hypothesis and *conjecture* are fancy words for "educated guess."

You may already have a hypothesis about what kind of quadrilateral the inner figure is. Be careful, though, because it may be that shape only for a particular shape of the outer quadrilateral. You need to convince yourself that your conjecture holds *no matter what shape the outer quadrilateral is.* This requires dragging. To gain even more confidence in your answer, you'll take measurements as well.

10. Drag various parts of the original quadrilateral around, keeping an eye on the inscribed figure.

11. Now, select the four inner segments and choose **Length** from the Measure menu.

    Four length measurements appear.

    m AB = 2.53 cm

12. Deselect all objects. Then select three consecutive midpoints and choose **Angle** from the Measure menu.

    An angle measurement appears beneath the length measurements. Notice that the vertex of the angle measured was the second *of the three points you selected.*

    m∠ABC = 84.61°

13. Select three consecutive midpoints again, with a different midpoint as the second selected point (vertex), and choose **Angle**. Repeat this step two more times, making sure a different midpoint is the second point selected each time.

    You should now have four angle measurements: one for each of the four angles of the inscribed quadrilateral.

The answer to our challenge—the word that fills in the blank—is in the illustration at the end of this tour.

14. Drag various parts of the original quadrilateral, making it wide, skinny, concave, and so on. What happens to the measurements? What changes and what stays the same? Are you more confident of your conjecture now? (As confident as you may feel, do you think you've *proven* the theorem?)

Creating a Caption and Using the Text Palette

To finish things off, let's create a caption for this sketch so that others who see it will know what's going on.

15. Choose the **Text** tool from the Toolbox.

16. Press-drag-release (or double-click) in a blank part of the sketch plane to start a new caption.

17. Use your keyboard to type the caption, perhaps stating your conjecture about the inner quadrilateral. Click outside the caption to close it. Drag the lower-right corner of the caption to adjust its margins.

To learn more about the various parts of the Text Palette, see the *Reference Manual* or Sketchpad's help system.

You may have noticed a new set of tools when working with captions (or other text objects). This is called the *Text Palette.* You can use the Text Palette to apply formatting options—such as italics, font size, font color, and more advanced mathematical formatting—to text. (You can manually show or hide the Text Palette using **Show Text Palette** or **Hide Text Palette** in the Display menu.)

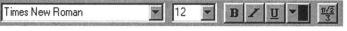

The Text Palette (Windows)

While you're exploring the Text Palette, you may also want to experiment with math notation. Click on the button on the far right of the Text Palette to show the math notation tools.

18. Use the Text Palette to change the font, text color, and other available settings of the caption. Changes will affect the entire caption because it's currently highlighted. Using the **Text** tool, click and drag within the caption to highlight a range of text and apply changes just to that text.

19. When you're ready, save your sketch.

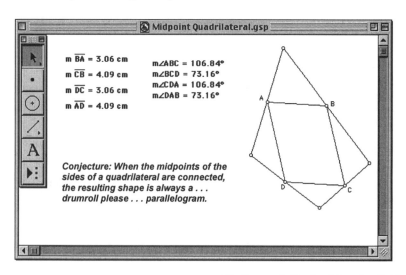

The Geometer's Sketchpad Learning Guide

Tour 3: String Art

The first two tours dealt with topics from traditional geometry. In later tours, you'll see that Sketchpad is just as useful in algebra, fractal geometry, and other areas. But some of the coolest things you can do with Sketchpad use mathematics in less traditional ways. In this tour, you'll learn about tracing and animation as you create some nifty Sketchpad versions of "string art."

What You Will Learn

- How to start a simple animation.

- How to use the Motion Controller to control an animation.

- How to trace an object.

- How to use the Context menu to access certain commands.

- How to create an Animation action button.

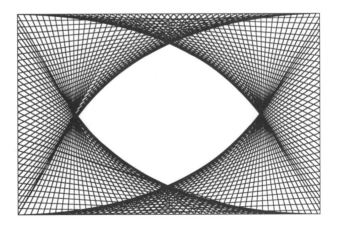

Selecting and Tracing

You'll find the **Tours** folder inside the **Samples** folder, which is in the same folder as the Sketchpad application itself

1. Open the sketch **String Art.gsp** from the **Tours** folder.

   You'll see two points constructed on a rectangle and connected by a yellow segment. The segment represents a piece of string. But instead of constructing more yellow segments to represent more pieces of string, you'll put the segment in motion and view its "traces."

2. Select the yellow segment by clicking on it with the **Arrow** tool.

3. Choose **Animate** from the Display menu.

   The segment begins moving around the rectangle. Also, the Motion Controller appears.

Note: The Mac Motion Controller looks a *little* bit different from the one at right.

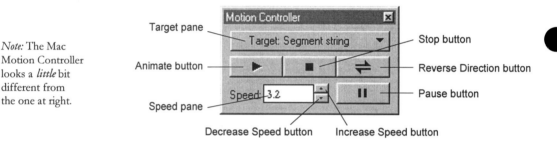

4. Try out the buttons on the Motion Controller. In particular, press the Increase Speed and Decrease Speed buttons and the Reverse Direction button. When you're ready, set the speed to a moderate level—about 3 or 4.

5. If the yellow segment is still selected, go on to the next step. If not, select it as follows: Press Pause on the Motion Controller; click in blank space in the sketch window to deselect all objects; select the yellow segment; then press Pause again to unpause.

6. Choose **Trace Segment** from the Display menu.

   You'll now see traces of the segment as it travels around the rectangle.

7. Let's see how things look with different colors. Choose a color from the Color submenu of the Display menu. (Bright colors work best against the dark background.)

   The segment's color changes, and as a result so does the color of its traces. Try out different colors until you find one you like.

The Geometer's Sketchpad Learning Guide

8. Experiment with the animation. Here are a few suggestions:

• Compare the animation when the two endpoints are close together with when they are far apart. You'll probably have to press the Pause button, drag an endpoint, then press Pause again to resume the animation.

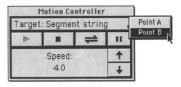

• Have one point move faster than the other. To target the Motion Controller's actions to a particular moving point, press the Target pane and hold down the mouse button as you drag and release over the desired point, as shown above right. Now a change in speed will affect only the targeted point.

You'll see that this isn't a true Sketchpad rectangle in that it fails the drag test! In this case, though, that's the way we wanted it to allow greater flexibility.

• Drag the rectangle's vertices to experiment with different shapes.

• Have the points move in opposite directions of each other. (*Hint:* Target only one point and reverse its direction using the Reverse Direction button.)

You've probably noticed that the traces gradually fade as the segment moves around the rectangle, allowing you to see the changing patterns without the screen getting too cluttered. But what if the traces are fading too slowly or quickly, or if you'd rather they not fade at all?

The two checkboxes at the bottom of the dialog box control whether changes apply to the current sketch or to all future sketches (or both). By default, only This Sketch is checked.

9. Choose **Preferences** from the Edit menu. Go to the Color panel by clicking on its tab near the top of the dialog box.

The Fade Traces Over Time checkbox controls whether or not traces fade. The slider to its right—available only when traces are set to fade—controls how quickly they fade.

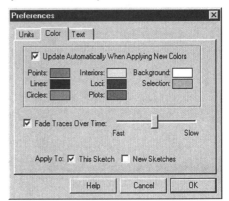

Color Preferences panel (Windows)

10. Experiment with having traces fade faster or slower or not at all. Here are a couple of tips:

The keyboard shortcut for **Erase Traces** is Ctrl+B (Windows) or ⌘+B (Mac).

- Try using the Context menu to get back into Preferences. In Windows, right-click over blank space to bring up the Context menu. On a Mac, hold down the Control key as you click in blank space.

- With traces set not to fade, you'll probably find that your rectangle quickly fills with color. Choose **Erase Traces** from the Display menu occasionally to start afresh.

Making an Animation Action Button

Using the **Animate** command or the Animate button on the Motion Controller are the easiest ways to start animations. But if there are particular patterns you like, with particular sets of speeds and direction settings, Animation *action buttons* give you more control.

11. Click in blank space to target all motions, then press the Stop button on the Motion Controller.

12. Deselect all objects, then select the "string" segment. Choose **Animation** from the Action Buttons submenu of the Edit menu.

    The Animate Properties dialog box appears.

Let's take a brief detour and ask, What if you didn't know what to do in a dialog box such as this one, or if you wanted to learn more about a topic? Sketchpad's help system to the rescue . . .

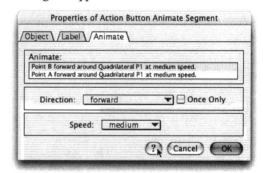

Animate Properties dialog box (Mac OS X)

You can also access the help system by choosing any of the commands in the Help menu.

13. Click the Help button ("Help" in Windows, "?" in Macintosh) to access the help topic for this command.

    Your default browser—Netscape® or Explorer® probably—launches and takes you to an appropriate page of Sketchpad's help system, which contains an electronic version of the complete Reference Manual. Spend a few moments navigating the help files to become acquainted with what's available.

The Geometer's Sketchpad Learning Guide

For more information on the various Speed and Direction settings, see the *Reference Manual* or Sketchpad's help system.

14. Return to Sketchpad (by choosing Sketchpad from the Application menu in the upper-right corner in Macintosh or from the Task Bar at the bottom of the screen in Windows). The Animate Properties dialog box will still be open. Choose Speed and Direction settings for points A and B—the two points that define the selected segment. When the settings are to your liking, click OK.

An Animation button appears. Press the button to start the animation. Press it again to stop the animation.

You can also get to the Properties dialog box of any object by right-clicking on it (Windows) or clicking on it while pressing the Control key (Mac).

15. Go ahead and make more Animation buttons with other settings. Or, to make changes to the existing button, select it (by clicking on the black band along its left edge) and choose **Properties** from the Edit menu.

All the Colors of the Rainbow: Parametric Color

Note: In this final section, we show you how to use one of Sketchpad's advanced features to add a rainbow of colors to your animation. If you'd rather stick to the basics, feel free to jump ahead to the next tour—we promise you won't miss anything essential!

If you've seen real string art, you know that one of the things that really adds to the effect is using a variety of colors. Here you'll use *parametric color* to color your segment according to its length. It's like coloring by numbers—as the number (length) changes, the color changes too.

16. If the segment is currently in motion, press the Pause button on the Motion Controller.

You need to give the measurement a bright color so it doesn't disappear against the black background!

17. Deselect all objects, then select the "string" segment. Choose **Length** from the Measure menu. With the measurement still selected, choose a bright color from the Color submenu of the Display menu.

18. Select both the length measurement and the segment that it's measuring. Choose **Parametric** from the Color submenu.

The Parametric Color dialog box appears.

Parametric Color dialog box (Mac)

19. Set the Parameter Domain to go from 0 to 2 and click OK.

20. Drag one endpoint of the segment so that its length gets longer and shorter. Its color changes! Notice that from a length of 0 to 2 units the segment takes on all of the colors in the rainbow.

Animations in which the two points are going at different speeds work best with this particular colorization.

21. Unpause the animation, press one of your animation buttons, or start a new animation.

22. Save your sketch. Take a break or just plow on ahead to Tour 4: A Bestiary of Quadrilaterals.

Tour 4: A Bestiary of Quadrilaterals

A *bestiary* is "a collection of descriptions of real or imaginary animals." Obviously, we're using the term a bit loosely!

When working in Sketchpad, you'll sometimes create your own sketches from scratch as you did in the first two tours. Other times you'll work with sketches—called *pre-made* sketches—someone else has put together, as in Tour 3. In this tour, you'll combine these two types of experience as you explore a pre-made sketch—a *multi-page document* in fact—and then add your own construction to it. To top things off, you'll learn how to turn constructions into easy-to-use tools.

What You Will Learn

- How to navigate through a multi-page document.

- How to show hidden objects (and hide them again).

- How to explore a construction using the Object Properties dialog box.

- How to add pages to a multi-page document.

- How to turn a construction into a custom tool, and how to then use that tool.

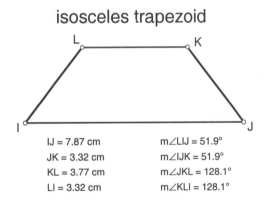

isosceles trapezoid

IJ = 7.87 cm	m∠LIJ = 51.9°
JK = 3.32 cm	m∠IJK = 51.9°
KL = 3.77 cm	m∠JKL = 128.1°
LI = 3.32 cm	m∠KLI = 128.1°

Navigating a Multi-page Document

1. Start Sketchpad (if it isn't already running) and choose **Open** from the File menu.

2. Find the **Tours** folder and open the sketch **Quadrilaterals.gsp**.

This document is called a *multi-page document* because it contains several "pages," just as many web sites contain many related pages. Think of it as a *sketchbook* for collecting several related sketches.

If you're connected to the Internet, you may also want to try pressing the button at the bottom of the TOC (table of contents)—it links to Sketchpad's home page on the World Wide Web!

3. Practice navigating through the sketchbook using both the link buttons, such as those at right, and the page tabs at the bottom of the window.

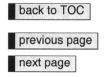

*To press a button, click on it with the **Arrow** tool.*

Exploring the Constructions

Try the following:

4. Go to the Isosceles Trapezoid page and drag point *L*.

What is the relationship between points L and K? What makes this trapezoid isosceles? Which measurements show that it's isosceles?

5. On the Rectangle page, drag points *E, H,* and *G* on the rectangle (one at a time).

How does the rectangle behave when each of these points is dragged?

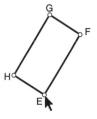

6. On the Parallelogram page, drag segments *MN* and *NO* (one at a time), keeping an eye on the measurements underneath.

What do you notice about angles and lengths in a parallelogram?

7. Experiment with dragging other points and segments. If any page becomes too "messy," just **Undo** repeatedly.

So, why do the quadrilaterals in our bestiary behave the way they do? What holds the rectangle together? Why do points *L* and *M* mirror each other the way they do? The techniques you'll use to explore these questions can be used to investigate other people's sketches in the future or to navigate your own constructions as they become more complicated.

Showing Hidden Objects and Exploring an Object's Properties

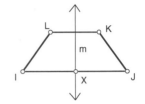

8. Go to the Isosceles Trapezoid page. Choose **Show All Hidden** from the Display menu.

   You now see a couple of objects—currently selected—that weren't visible before.

9. Click in a blank part of the sketch to deselect all objects.

10. Drag the various parts of the sketch around.

    How do the objects in this sketch relate to line m? Where is point X located along segment IJ?

11. Deselect all objects, then select line *m* by clicking on it. Choose **Properties** from the Edit menu.

    If you see something different from what's shown below, try clicking on the Object tab near the top of the dialog box.

Object Properties panel (Windows)

Take a few moments to read the description of line *m*. This line was evidently constructed using the **Perpendicular Line** command with segment *IJ* and point *X* selected. Notice too that the Hidden checkbox is unchecked, meaning that line *m* is currently showing. You could hide it by checking this box. Similarly, line *m* is arrow selectable—meaning that clicking on it with the **Arrow** tool selects it.

12. Move the Properties dialog box (drag it by its title bar) until you can see all of the objects in the sketch below.

An object's parents are what define the object—the objects its construction was based on. Its children are those things that are defined by the object.

13. Press on the Parents pop-up menu and highlight one and then the other choice (don't release the mouse button yet).

The listed objects highlight in the sketch when they're highlighted in this menu. Note that the two objects listed in the Parents menu are the same two from the object description.

14. Release the mouse button over one of line *m*'s two parents.

The Object panel switches to describe the chosen point.

You can also change an object's label, and whether or not the label is showing, in the Label panel. Just click the Label tab near the top of the dialog box. Other panels may appear in Properties for other types of objects.

15. Continue "navigating the family tree." See if you can get to every object's Object panel, including those of the measurements. Pay attention to each object's description and think about why it has the parents and children it does and why the construction works.

You'll need to use the Children pop-up menu here as well.

16. When you're ready to move on, click OK.

Adding a Page to the Document

These next two sections are about laziness . . . uh . . . make that *resourcefulness.* You constructed a square in a previous tour, and while it may be in your best interest to practice making more squares, you'll now learn how to get the most mileage out of that one effort.

Notice first that our sketchbook calls itself a "Bestiary of Quadrilaterals" and yet it doesn't even contain the most perfect quadrilateral of all—the square! We'll fix that now.

17. If your sketch from Tour 1 (probably called **Square.gsp**) is still open, skip to the next step. Otherwise, choose **Open** from the File menu, navigate until this file is highlighted, and click Open.

18. Click somewhere in **Quadrilaterals.gsp** to make it the active document once again.

19. Choose **Document Options** from the File menu.

The Document Options dialog box appears.

You can change the order of pages in the document by dragging them in the Document Pages list. You can also rename pages in the Page Name field or remove pages using the Remove Page button.

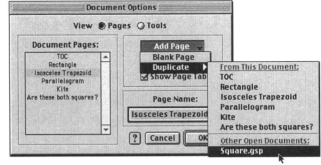

Document Options dialog box (Mac)

20. Add **Square.gsp** to the sketchbook by choosing it from the Add Page pop-up menu, as shown above. Then click OK.

Open the new page by clicking on its tab at the bottom of the sketch window. If you don't see this particular tab, press the arrows to the right and left of the tabs to scroll through all of the page tabs.

Making Your Square into a Custom Tool

If you needed to construct several more squares, it might get a little tedious doing the same steps over and over. Wouldn't it be nice if there were a special tool just for constructing squares? In fact, you can turn almost any of your constructions into a custom tool—available right from the Toolbox—that re-creates the construction in just a few clicks. Here's how.

21. On the Square page, make sure the **Arrow** tool is chosen. Now choose **Select All** from the Edit menu.

Step 22

22. Choose **Create New Tool** from the Custom Tools menu in the Toolbox. Enter the name Square and click OK.

The new tool will now be listed at the bottom of the Custom Tools menu, as shown at right.

After step 22

23. Click on the Custom Tools icon in the Toolbox to choose the most recently created tool—in this case **Square**.

The cursor becomes a white arrow with a point at its tip.

24. Click the mouse button anywhere in the sketch plane to construct one corner of the square. Now move the tool to where you'd like the second corner to be and click again.

*Your tool constructs a square defined by the two points created where you clicked. The **Square** tool is still active, ready to keep constructing squares until you choose a different tool.*

25. Practice using the tool to construct squares. Notice that the direction in which the square is constructed depends on the relative locations of the two clicks. Try each of the following:

- Construct a square by clicking from left to right.

- Construct a square by clicking from right to left.

- Hold down the Shift key while you use the tool. This limits segment slopes to 15° increments, making it easy to construct perfectly horizontal or vertical segments.

- Experiment with **Undo**. (Notice that it undoes the tool's entire construction.)

- By clicking on existing points or other objects, you can construct squares that are "attached" to these objects. Try using your **Square** tool (and nothing else) to construct the figure below. See what other patterns you can create!

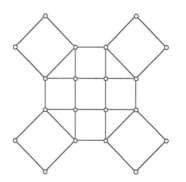

The Geometer's Sketchpad Learning Guide

Tours 5–6: Transformations

Transformational geometry explores how figures can be turned,
flipped, slid, stretched, or squeezed. In this pair of tours, you'll explore
some of these transformations using Sketchpad's Transform menu.
You'll start by investigating a fundamental problem having to do with
reflections and rotations. Then you'll create a simple kaleidoscope.
Along the way, you'll learn a little more about the Measure menu and
custom tools.

Tour 5: Reflection + Reflection = ?

In this tour, you'll investigate a topic from transformational geometry and see how Sketchpad can really make it come alive.

What You Will Learn

- How to quickly construct a general polygon interior.

- How to reflect objects across "mirror lines."

- How to use Sketchpad's Calculator.

- How to rotate an object around a marked point and by a marked angle or calculation.

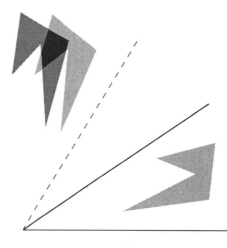

Introduction

Sketchpad's Transform menu has commands for the following four basic transformations:

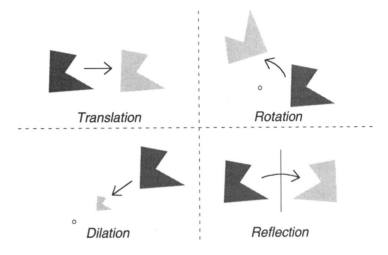

Translation | Rotation

Dilation | Reflection

Are any of these four transformations *more basic* than the others? In other words, can any of them be accomplished by combining others? For example, can multiple translations result in a rotation? The answer is no because a rotation *turns* an object, whereas translations do not involve turning. Can multiple rotations result in a dilation? Again, the answer is no because a dilation involves a *size* change, whereas rotations preserve size. But can multiple reflections, across different lines, result in a rotation? This does seem possible, and in this tour you'll explore that possibility.

Actually, in some special cases dilations and rotations are equivalent. For example, a dilation by a scale factor of –1 is equivalent to a rotation of 180°.

Constructing the Mirrors and the Polygon Interior

Remember: If you get stuck at any point in this tour, just open **Tour5_StepByStep.gsp** in the **Tours** folder (which is inside the **Samples** folder next to the application itself). There are StepByStep sketches for most tours.

You'll start by constructing the two segments that will serve as the "mirrors" and the polygon interior that will be reflected over them.

1. In a new sketch, use the **Segment** tool to draw a segment.

2. Draw a second segment that shares one endpoint with the first.

   We'll refer to this figure as "the V."

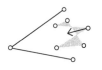

After step 2

A "general polygon" is a polygon with no special properties, such as congruent sides or right angles. You'll see how easy it is to quickly construct one in the next two steps.

Holding down the Shift key tells Sketchpad to keep previously constructed objects selected.

3. Choose the **Point** tool and click inside the V to draw a point. Hold down the Shift key and draw four more points nearby.

   You should now have five points, all selected, inside the V.

Note that when constructing a polygon interior, you don't select the sides of the polygon, just the vertices.

4. Choose **Pentagon Interior** from the Construct menu.

   If your polygon folds over itself, drag the vertex points until it appears whole, as shown at right.

Step 4: Drag the point as indicated to get a single, well-defined polygon.

Marking Mirrors and Reflecting over Them

Now, to explore the question we began with, you'll reflect the interior over one of the V's segments, then reflect the result over the other segment.

5. Select the lower segment and choose **Mark Mirror** from the Transform menu.

   A brief animation indicates that the segment has been marked as a mirror for subsequent reflections.

6. Select the polygon interior (by clicking on the shape itself) and choose **Reflect** from the Transform menu.

The reflected image of the interior appears across the mirror.

Things will look best in this tour and the next if you use light colors.

7. With the reflected interior still selected, choose a different color from the Color submenu of the Display menu. Then double-click the upper segment to mark it as the new mirror.

This is an alternate way to mark a mirror.

8. Choose **Reflect** again to reflect the selected pentagon interior over the newly marked mirror. Give this second reflected image a different color.

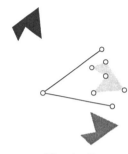

9. Drag a point on the original interior and observe the effect on the mirror images. Drag other objects in the sketch as well.

Take a moment to examine your sketch. How does the third polygon appear to relate to the original polygon?

After step 8

You may have noticed that the third polygon appears to be a *rotation* of the original polygon. To test this conjecture, you'll now rotate the original polygon until it is on top of the third polygon. Then you'll investigate further using measurements.

Marking, Rotating, and Measuring

10. Choose the **Segment** tool. Construct a third segment, just outside the V, that shares the same vertex point, as shown below.

11. With the segment selected, choose **Dashed** from the Line Width submenu of the Display menu.

The dashed line width distinguishes the new segment from the original two.

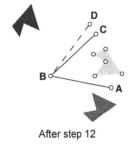

12. Using the **Text** tool, click on the four segment endpoints in the (alphabetical) order shown at right.

After step 12

The goal in the next several steps is to rotate the original interior the same amount as the larger angle just created (∠*ABD*). You'll start by *marking* this angle, just as you previously marked a mirror.

Note that when marking angles, as with measuring them, you select the vertex point *second.* The marked angle is directed from the first point, around the vertex (second point), toward the third point.

13. Deselect all objects. Then select the three points defining the new larger angle in the following order: point *A* first, point *B* second, and point *D* third.

14. With these three points selected, choose **Mark Angle** from the Transform menu.

    A brief animation indicates that the angle has been marked for subsequent rotations.

15. Select the common endpoint of the segments (point *B*), and choose **Mark Center** from the Transform menu.

    A brief animation indicates that the point has been marked as a center for subsequent rotations (or dilations).

16. Select the original interior and choose **Rotate** from the Transform menu. Make sure the By Marked Angle option is chosen, then click Rotate.

    A rotated image appears, rotated by the measure of the angle you marked in the previous step.

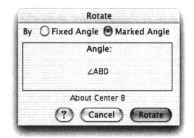

Rotate dialog box (Mac OS X)

The new interior moves as you drag point *D.* Why? Because this changes the marked angle that *defined* that rotation.

17. Drag point *D* until the new interior and the second reflected image coincide.

How does the angle between the mirror lines (the original V, ∠*ABC*) compare to the angle of rotation for the newest interior (the larger V, ∠*ABD*)? Make a conjecture before proceeding.

18. Measure the V angle (∠*ABC*). To do this, select the three points defining the angle and choose **Angle** from the Measure menu. Make sure to select the vertex (point *B*) second.

    The angle measurement appears.

19. Use the same technique to measure the larger angle, ∠*ABD*.

    Does your conjecture appear to be correct? Drag points to explore related cases.

m∠ABC = 45.52°
m∠ABD = 61.39°

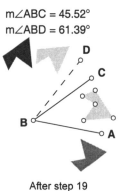

After step 19

Rotating by a Marked Calculation

You probably found that the larger angle is twice the smaller when the two interiors coincide. You could just pack your bags and move on. But to be more certain of your conclusion—and to get an introduction to Sketchpad's Calculator—you'll continue by rotating the original interior by an amount calculated to be *exactly* twice the angle of the V.

20. Select point D and press the Delete key (Mac) or Backspace key (Windows).

The point disappears and so do its children (the objects defined by it): the dashed segment, the newest interior, and the second angle measurement.

You may need to drag the New Calculation dialog box out of the way to see and click on the measurement.

21. Calculate twice the angle measurement of the V. To do this, choose **Calculate** from the Measure menu. Then type a 2, click on the angle measurement in the sketch, and click OK.

Earlier in this tour, you used **Mark Angle** with three points selected. You can also mark an angle calculation or measurement, as you do here.

22. With the new calculation still selected, choose **Mark Angle**.

A brief animation indicates that the angle calculation has been marked for subsequent rotations.

23. Rotate the original interior by the marked, calculated angle.

See step 16 if you need a reminder how to do this.

The Calculator (Windows)

The newly rotated interior lands right on top of the doubly-reflected interior. This demonstrates that a rotation can be thought of as a composition of two reflections over intersecting lines. Such a rotation is centered at the point of intersection of the two mirror lines and the angle of rotation is twice the angle between them.

Finally, you'll prepare your sketch for the next tour.

24. Select the calculation $(2 \cdot m\angle ABC = \ldots)$ and press the Delete key (Mac) or Backspace key (Windows).

25. If you're planning to take a break before moving on to the next tour, make sure to save the current sketch in a convenient place because you'll need it to build your kaleidoscope in Tour 6.

Tour 6: Building a Kaleidoscope

In the previous tour, you reflected a polygon interior across two segments. What if you did the same thing to the final image—reflected it across the same two segments—and then kept on doing this over and over to each new result? What patterns would emerge? How would they relate to the angle between the segments? You'll start this tour by building a custom tool to explore this question. Then comes the fun part—building a kaleidoscope. You'll learn about dilating and merging points to paths as you turn your figure into an animated kaleidoscope like the one below.

What You Will Learn

- How to create a custom tool that defines a multi-step transformation.

- How to dilate objects about a marked center.

- How to merge independent points to paths.

Defining and Using a New Custom Tool

In Tour 4, you turned an earlier square construction into a tool for quickly constructing new squares. Here you'll create a more sophisticated tool, one that reflects any given object across two given straight objects, resulting in two reflected images.

For a more complete description of custom tools, see the Reference Manual or Sketchpad's help system.

A custom tool, as you've seen, provides a way to apply an existing construction to new objects. To define a custom tool, you start by creating the construction itself. Then you select the *givens* of the construction (the objects the construction is based on) and the *results* (the objects you wish the construction to produce). In this case, the givens are the original interior and the two mirror lines. The results of your tool are the two interiors that resulted from reflecting the given interior over the two given mirror lines.

1. If it isn't still open, open your sketch from the previous tour.

2. Drag one of the endpoints of the V until the angle measures close to 45°.

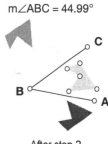

m∠ABC = 44.99°

After step 2

The order you select givens when defining a tool determines the order you'll click objects when using the tool (as you'll do in step 5). The order you select results doesn't matter.

3. Select your desired givens (first the original interior, then segment *AB,* then segment *BC*) and then your desired results (the two reflected interiors).

   You should have five objects selected.

4. Choose **Create New Tool** from the Custom Tools menu in the Toolbox. Enter the name `Double Reflection` and click OK.

   The new custom tool will now be listed at the bottom of the Custom Tools menu, as shown at right.

Step 4

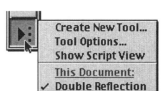

5. Click on the Custom Tools icon in the Toolbox to choose the most recently created tool—in this case **Double Reflection**. Click on the upper-left polygon interior, then the lower segment, then the upper segment.

   Two more interiors appear. Notice that what was done to the original interior—being reflected over the two segments—has now been done to the clicked-on interior.

You'll know you're about to match an interior when its perimeter highlights.

6. The custom tool is still active. Click this time on the last interior constructed by the tool (the one that's the same color as what we've been calling the upper-left interior) and again on the two segments.

   You now should have seven polygons, as shown at right.

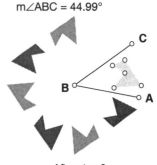

m∠ABC = 44.99°

After step 6

7. Choose **Undo** from the Edit menu twice. Notice that one entire **Double Reflection** is undone each time. Now choose **Redo** twice to return to the previous state.

8. Drag one of the vertices of the original polygon to see the effect on the six other polygons.

9. Locate the interior that's directly across from what we've called the upper-left interior. Keep an eye on it as you drag point *C* to make the angle something less "round" than 45° (such as 48° or 83°). Keep using the **Double Reflection** tool until there are 25–30 interiors. Start by clicking on the interior you had your eye on, then segment *AB,* then segment *BC.* In each case, after one of these three-click cycles, continue by clicking on the most recently constructed interior (it will be highlighted).

   This is a very tricky step. If you get stuck, remember that you can go to the "after step 9" page of **Tour6_StepByStep** *(located in the* **Sketchpad | Samples | Tours** *folder) and proceed from there.*

Experimenting with the Mirror Angle

To control the mirror angle precisely, drag the mirror endpoint far away from the vertex point; then use the arrow keys on your keyboard to drag one pixel at a time.

10. Play with the mirror angle. Note that for certain angles, many of the interiors are *coincident* (right on top of each other). Try 60°, 36°, 30°, and 90° to see some examples.

Can you state a conjecture as to why certain angles have this special property? Can you predict how many interiors there will appear to be for a given one of these special angles? (The answers are at the end of this tour.)

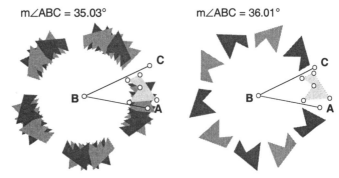

m∠ABC = 35.03°   m∠ABC = 36.01°

Step 10 for two different angles

When you've finished exploring this question, you'll continue with your kaleidoscope.

11. Using the keyboard shortcut for **Undo** (Ctrl+Z or ⌘+Z), undo back to the point at which there were just seven interiors.

12. Drag so that the V angle is as close to 60° as you can make it.

13. Use the **Hide** command from the Display menu to hide the original interior. The easiest way to select this interior (since it's "beneath" another at the moment) is to select one of its vertex points and choose **Select Children** from the Edit menu.

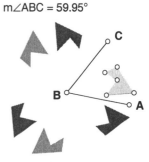

m∠ABC = 59.95°

After step 13

Dilating

Real-life kaleido-
scopes don't involve
dilations, but you'll
dilate here to give
your kaleidoscope
extra flair.

The **Dilate** command shrinks objects toward or stretches them away
from a marked center by a specified scale factor. A negative scale
factor will dilate the object right through the center point and out
the other side!

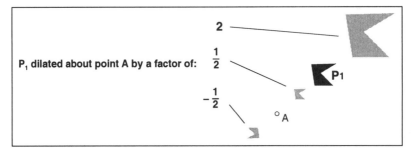

P_1 dilated about point A by a factor of: 2 $\dfrac{1}{2}$ $-\dfrac{1}{2}$

14. Double-click point B to mark it as a center for subsequent
transformations.

15. Select three interiors with the
same color and choose **Dilate**
from the Transform menu.

The Dilate dialog box appears.

16. Enter –1/2 for the scale
factor, as shown at right,
and click Dilate.

*Three dilated images
appear, each 1/2 the size of
its pre-image. Also, because
of the negative scale factor,*
each image is on the side of the center point opposite its pre-image.

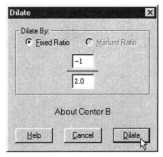

Dilate dialog box (Windows)

17. With the three new interiors selected, choose a new color from the
Color submenu of the Display menu.

18. With the three interiors still selected, choose **Dilate** again. Click
Dilate to use the same scale factor. Give the three newest interiors
a different color.

19. Select the other three of the original six interiors (the three you didn't select in step 15) and repeat steps 15–18.

    When you're done, you should have 18 interiors—3 each of 6 different colors—as shown at right.

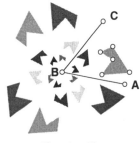

m∠ABC = 59.95°

After step 19

20. Drag one or more of the vertices of the original interior to see how everything else in the sketch changes accordingly.

Animating and Merging

21. Select any interior in the sketch and choose **Animate** from the Display menu.

The points that define the interior you selected—the five vertices of the original polygon—are *independent* points. (This means that they were drawn in blank space instead of constructed on an object or defined in some other way.) Independent points—and objects descended from them—animate *randomly* in the plane, as you can see. You can gain more control over these animating points by first *merging* them to existing and newly created paths.

22. Click the Stop button in the Motion Controller (or choose **Stop Animation** from the Display menu).

There are many more uses for the **Merge** command than what is covered here. You can, for example, merge measurements and captions. Also, in some situations **Merge** becomes **Split**. Among other things, you can use **Split** to split points from their paths and make them independent points.

23. Select one of the vertex points and one of the segments and choose **Merge Point To Segment** from the Edit menu.

    The point attaches itself to the segment. Try dragging it and you'll see that it can now move only along its new segment path.

24. Use the same technique to merge a second vertex point to the other segment.

25. Use the **Compass** tool to create three circles of any size anywhere in your sketch. (Make sure to click only in blank space—don't attach the circles to any existing objects.)

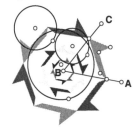

After step 25

26. Now merge, one by one, the remaining three vertex points to the three circles.

    Each vertex point should now be attached to a different segment or circular path.

27. Select any interior and choose **Animate**.

    Each vertex starts animating along its path.

28. Use the Motion Controller to fine tune your kaleidoscope. Remember that you can target individual points by pressing on the Target pane near the top of the Motion Controller. Try changing the speeds and directions of several of the points. You can also drag points to change the size and location of the path objects in the sketch.

29. When you're pleased with your kaleidoscope, hide everything but the interiors. Here's a quick way to do that:

    - Deselect all objects.

    - Choose the **Point** tool, then choose **Select All Points** from the Edit menu.

    - Choose **Hide Points** from the Display menu.

    - Repeat the last two sub-steps, first with the **Compass** tool, then with the **Segment** tool.

Answers to questions from step 10: Interiors will "line up" for mirror angles that are factors of 360°. The number of apparent interiors will be 360° divided by the mirror angle (or a multiple of this). For example, for a mirror angle of 36°, there appear to be 10 (360° ÷ 36°) interiors.

The Geometer's Sketchpad Learning Guide

Tour 7: Algebra Potpourri

Don't let the name of the program—The *Geometer's* Sketchpad—fool you. Sketchpad has a host of tools for exploring algebra, trigonometry, and calculus, both symbolically (with equations) and graphically. In this tour, you'll sample several of Sketchpad's algebra features.

What You Will Learn

- How to create an *x-y* coordinate system and measure the coordinates of a point.

- How to define and plot functions.

- How to plot two measurements as an (*x, y*) point in the plane.

- How to construct a locus.

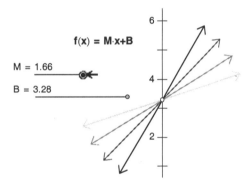

A Simple Plot in the Coordinate (*x-y*) Plane

At the heart of "visual" algebra is the *x-y* plane, also know as the *Cartesian* plane or the *coordinate* plane. In this section, you'll define a coordinate plane, measure a point's coordinates on it, and plot a simple function.

1. Open a new sketch and choose **Define Coordinate System** from the Graph menu.

   A standard coordinate system is created—a square x-y grid with its origin in the center of the sketch window.

2. Using the **Point** tool, create a point somewhere other than on an axis.

3. With the point still selected, choose **Coordinates** from the Measure menu.

The point is labeled A and its coordinates are displayed. Drag the point around to change its coordinates.

You can plot a function without first creating a coordinate system. Sketchpad creates coordinate systems automatically whenever needed.

Now that there's a coordinate system, let's plot a simple equation on it: $y = x$.

4. Choose **Plot New Function** from the Graph menu.

The New Function dialog box appears.

5. Click x on the dialog box keypad (or type x from your keyboard). Click OK.

The function equation $f(x) = x$ appears along with a plot of its graph, $y = x$.

6. Select the plot you just created and the independent point (whose coordinates you measured). Then choose **Merge Point To Function Plot**.

New Function dialog box (Windows)

The point attaches itself to the function plot. Drag the point along the plot and observe its coordinates—the x- and y-coordinates always equal each other (not surprising for the plot of "y equals x"!).

You may notice when changing the scale in step 7 that the plot's domain is restricted. If you'd like to change the domain, either drag the arrows at either end or select the plot, choose **Properties**, and change the domain on the Plot panel.

7. Drag any tick-mark number or the unit point at (1, 0) to the right and left; observe how the coordinate system scale changes.

The axis numbers and the grid itself update automatically.

8. Move the unit point back so that the x-axis goes from around –10 to 10.

Plotting a Family of Curves with Parameters

Plotting one particular equation, $y = x$, is all well and good. But the real power of Sketchpad comes when you plot *families* of equations, such as the family of lines of the form $y = mx + b$. You'll start by defining parameters m and b and editing the existing function equation to include the new parameters. Then you'll *animate* the parameters to see a dynamic representation of this family of lines.

As you can see, a parameter is a type of variable that takes on a fixed value.

9. Choose **New Parameter** from the Graph menu. Enter m for Name and 2 for Value and click OK.

10. Use the same technique to create a parameter *b* with the value −1.

Edit Function appears as **Edit Calculation**, **Edit Parameter**, or **Edit Plotted Point** when one of those types of objects is selected. Double-clicking a function equation, calculation, or parameter brings up the same dialog box, as does using the keyboard shortcut ⌘+E (Mac) or Ctrl+E (Windows).

New Parameter dialog box (Mac OS X)

11. Select the function equation $f(x) = x$ (select the equation itself, not its plot) and choose **Edit Function** from the Edit menu.

The Edit Function dialog box appears.

12. Edit the function to be $f(x) = m \cdot x + b$. (Click on the parameters *m* and *b* in the sketch to enter them. Use * (Shift+8) for multiplication.) Click OK.

The function equation and its associated plot both update. The plot you see is y = 2x − 1, which is y = mx + b for m = 2 and b = −1.

13. Change *m* and *b* (by double-clicking them) to explore several different graphs in the form $y = mx + b$, such as $y = 5x + 2$, $y = -1x - 7$, and $y = 0.5x$.

Hint: To plot y = 0.5x, set b to 0.

You can learn a lot by changing the parameters manually, as you did in the previous step. But it can be especially revealing to watch the plot as its parameters change smoothly or in steps.

14. Deselect all objects. Then select the parameter equation for *m* and choose **Animate Parameter** from the Display menu.

The value for m begins increasing ("animating") and the plotted line changes accordingly. Also, the Motion Controller appears. Use the Motion Controller to change the speed and "direction" m changes. (See page 26 to review the Motion Controller buttons.)

15. Press the Stop button to stop the animation.

16. Select *m* and choose **Properties** from the Edit menu. Go to the Parameter panel and change the settings so they resemble those at right. Click OK.

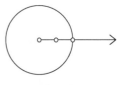

The Parameter Properties dialog box (Windows)

17. Again choose **Animate Parameter**.

How does this parameter animation compare with the previous one?

18. Continue experimenting with parameter animation. You might try, among other things, animating both parameters simultaneously or tracing the line as it moves in the plane.

Functions in a Circle

How does the radius of a circle relate to its circumference? To its area? These are examples of geometric relationships that can also be thought of as functions and studied algebraically.

You'll start by constructing a circle whose radius adjusts continuously along a straight path.

To choose the **Ray** tool, press the current **Straightedge** tool in the Toolbox and select it from the palette that appears.

19. In a new sketch, use the **Ray** tool to construct a horizontal ray.

Holding down the Shift key helps keep the ray horizontal.

20. With the ray still selected, choose **Point On Ray** from the Construct menu.

*A point is constructed somewhere on the ray, just as if you had clicked on that spot with the **Point** tool.*

21. With the **Arrow** tool, click in blank space to deselect all objects. Then select, in order, the ray's endpoint and the point constructed in step 20. Choose **Circle By Center+Point** from the Construct menu.

Step 21

*A circle appears, centered at the first selected point and passing through the second. (Note that steps 20 and 21 could also have been accomplished using the **Compass** tool.)*

In each case, use the **Arrow** tool to select the circle (and nothing else), then choose the appropriate command in the Measure menu.

22. Measure the circle's radius, circumference, and area.

23. Drag the circle's radius point and watch the measurements change.

    Can you describe how the circumference and area measurements change? What's different about the way they change? You'll now explore these questions by plotting.

24. Select, in order, the radius measurement and the circumference measurement. Choose **Plot As (x, y)** from the Graph menu.

    A coordinate system is created and a point is plotted. If you can't see the point yet, it's most likely plotted off the screen.

In a *rectangular grid,* the *x-* and *y-*axes can be scaled independently.

25. Choose **Rectangular Grid** from the Graph | Grid Form submenu. Drag the new unit point at (0, 1) down until you can see the plotted point from step 24.

    Notice that the point's x-coordinate is the radius of the circle and its y-coordinate is the circumference. This is because of how the point was constructed in step 24.

Choose **Erase Traces** from the Display menu to erase this trace at any time.

26. Select the plotted point and choose **Trace Plotted Point** from the Display menu. Drag the radius point and observe the trace.

In situations such as this (where you trace something as a point moves along a path) you can often get a smoother picture by creating a locus.

27. Select the plotted point and the radius point; then choose **Locus** from the Construct menu.

    A locus is plotted—the set of all possible locations of the plotted point as the radius point moves along its path.

More accurately, a Sketchpad locus is a *sample* of possible locations of the selected object. To change the number of samples plotted, select the locus, choose **Properties** from the Edit menu, and go to the Plot panel.

28. Repeat steps 24 and 27, except this time explore the relationship between the radius and area measurements.

    You should now have two loci, one for the radius-circumference relationship and one for the radius-area relationship. How do these curves compare? For what radius does a circle's circumference equal its area?

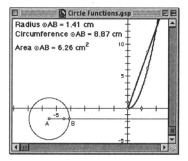

This is just a small sampling of Sketchpad's algebra capabilities. To learn more, check out the *Reference Manual* (particularly the Graph menu chapter) or Sketchpad's help system.

Tour 8: Constructing a Snowflake—Iteration

Note: Iteration is a rich mathematical subject, so don't worry if you don't understand all the finer points the first time through. We hope that upon completing the tour you'll be inspired to experiment, read further, and become more and more comfortable with this feature.

Iteration allows you to apply constructions, transformations, or other operations over and over again. It can be used not only to save time on constructions that involve repeated steps, but also to create figures such as intricate fractals. (A *fractal,* roughly speaking, is a figure that looks the same when viewed at different magnifications. The parts, in other words, are scale copies of the whole.)

In this tour, you'll start with a construction involving dilation and rotation. You'll then use the **Iterate** command to apply the same construction to smaller parts of the figure. The result of this process is a fractal called the *Koch curve.* Once you've constructed the Koch curve, you'll do a second iteration to construct the interior of the curve. You'll then turn the entire figure into a custom tool that you'll apply to the three vertices of an equilateral triangle, creating a beautiful shape called a *Koch snowflake.*

What You Will Learn

- How to use Sketchpad's **Iterate** command.

- How to change the appearance of iterated images.

- How to change the number of iterations in an iterated image.

- How to change the background color of a sketch.

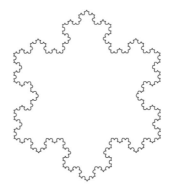

Understanding the Koch Curve

Before getting started, it's worth understanding what the Koch curve is and how it's formed. It was first described by Helge von Koch in 1904, long before there was a branch of mathematics called "fractal geometry." Koch studied the curve that came to bear his name to show that *a curve that fits in a finite region of space can be infinitely long.* Here's how it works:

- Start with two points.

- Connect these points with a segment and divide the segment into thirds.

- Remove the middle third and construct the top two sides of an equilateral triangle above the missing section.

The mathematical term for "do the same thing" is *iterate.* The fourth figure at right is the first *iteration* of the previous operation.

- Do the same thing to each of the four smaller segments formed.

- Keep performing the construction on smaller and smaller segments (to infinity, in theory).

So, how does the result of this process show that a curve fitting in a finite region can be infinitely long? Well, at each stage of the construction, the curve is longer than at the previous stage. (Can you see by how much?) If the process were carried out infinitely many times, you'd end up with an infinitely long curve that fits in a finite area!

Of course, Sketchpad can't carry out an iteration infinitely many times, but it can iterate enough times to reveal the structure of the Koch curve and other fractals. In this tour, you'll experiment with different depths of iteration, and you'll see that it doesn't take too many to get a very finely detailed approximation of the Koch curve.

Laying the Groundwork

The first step in any iteration is to actually do the basic operations you wish to later repeat by iterating. In this case, that means "dividing" a segment in three and building an equilateral triangle over the middle third, as described on the previous page.

1. In a new sketch, choose **Preferences** from the Edit menu. On the Text page, choose For All New Points and click OK.

   Points will now be automatically labeled as you create them.

2. Use the **Segment** tool to construct a horizontal segment from left to right in the sketch window. Hold down the Shift key while constructing the segment to keep it horizontal.

   A ○————————————○ B

   After step 2

3. Select point *B* and choose **Mark Center** from the Transform menu.

4. Select point *A* and choose **Dilate** from the Transform menu. Leave the numerator of the Scale Factor 1 and enter 3 for its denominator, as shown at right. Click OK.

   A point is constructed 1/3 of the way from point B to point A.

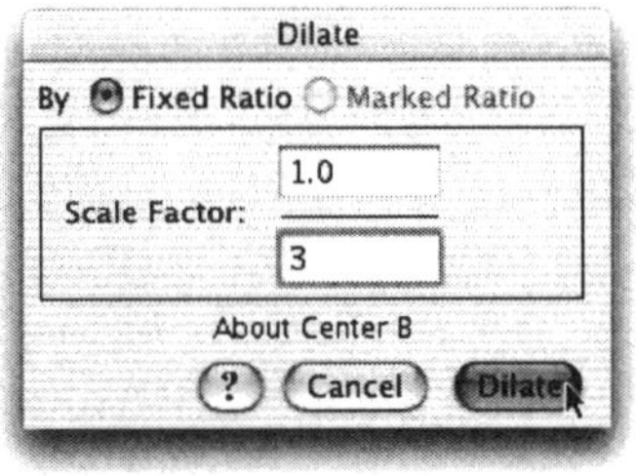

   Dilate dialog box (Mac OS X)

5. Repeat steps 3 and 4, except this time dilate point *B* 1/3 of its distance from point *A*.

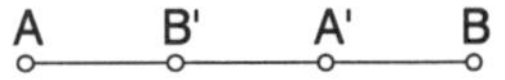

   A ○——B'○——A'○——○ B

   After step 5

6. Double-click point *B'* to mark it as a center.

7. Select point *A'* and choose **Rotate** from the Transform menu. Enter 60 for the angle, as shown at right, and click Rotate.

   A point appears above the others.

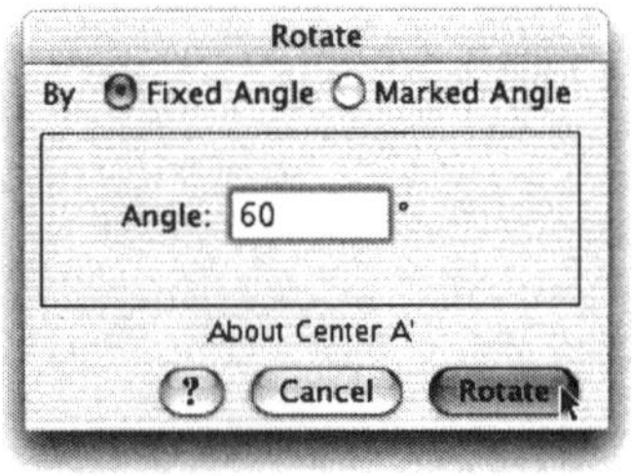

   Rotate dialog box (Mac OS X)

8. Hide the original segment connecting the left and right points.

The Geometer's Sketchpad Learning Guide

9. Use the **Segment** tool to connect the five points with segments, as shown below right.

10. Relabel the three middle points to match the figure at right. To change a label, double-click the label itself with the **Arrow** or **Text** tool.

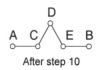

After step 10

Iterating

Think for a moment about what you've "done" to points A and B: Initially there was a segment between them, but then you did some transformations and hid that original segment. Now imagine doing the same things to points A and C—doing the same transformations on them and then hiding the segment between them. Imagine also doing these things to points C and D, D and E, and E and B. This is precisely what you'll do in the next several steps. Thinking about it in this way should help you understand what's going on.

11. Select points A and B and choose **Iterate** from the Transform menu.

The Iterate dialog box appears, prompting you to match A and B.

Step 12: Clicking on point *A* to map it to itself

12. You want to do to points A and C what you did to points A and B. So click on point A in the sketch to map point A to itself, as shown above. Then click on point C to map point B to point C.

You should see A and C under First Image in the Iterate dialog box.

13. Choose **Add New Map** from the Structure pop-up menu in the Iterate dialog box.

    A second map appears, prompting you to once again map A and B to new points.

14. This time, click on points *C* and *D* to do to points *C* and *D* what you did to points *A* and *B*.

The keyboard shortcut for **Add New Map** is ⌘+A (Mac) or Ctrl+A (Windows).

15. Repeat steps 13 and 14 once for points *D* and *E* and again for points *E* and *B*.

You're almost ready to click Iterate, but notice in the preview in the sketch that the larger segments weren't hidden from iteration level to iteration level. The next step will fix this. (If you're not sure what we're talking about here, just do the next step and observe the effect this has on the sketch.)

16. Choose **Final Iteration Only** from the Display submenu of the Iterate dialog box.

17. Your Iterate dialog box should look like the one below. If it does, click Iterate. If it doesn't, highlight any boxes that are different and click on the proper points.

18. Hide the four original segments.

Congratulations! You've constructed a fractal—the Koch curve (or, more precisely, an *iterated approximation* of this curve). Drag points *A* and *B* to get a better idea of how it's constructed.

The Geometer's Sketchpad Learning Guide

Iteration Depth, Background Color, and "Full Orbit" Iteration

By default, Sketchpad repeated the iteration three times. You can change the number—or "depth"—of iteration to change the curve. Here's how:

You can use the + or − keys on your standard keyboard or those on your numeric keypad (if you have one).

19. Select any part of the iterated image and press the + and − keys on your keyboard.

This increases and decreases the number of iterations.

20. Return to iteration depth 3. The easiest way to do this is to press the − key over and over until nothing changes—this is depth 1. Now press the + key twice to get to depth 3.

We promised that you'd be creating a snowflake, so it only makes sense to work against a blue background.

21. Open the Preferences dialog box and go to the Color panel. Click on the Background color swatch. Use the controls to get a nice shade of sky blue. Click OK twice.

Now you'll create a second iterated image of white polygon interiors that will form the snowflake itself.

22. Select points *C, D,* and *E* and choose **Triangle Interior** from the Construct menu.

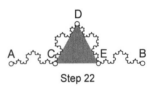

Step 22

23. With the new interior selected, choose **Display | Color | Other.** Use the controls there to produce white and click OK.

24. Repeat steps 11–15. (Don't choose **Final Iteration Only**, as in step 16: You *do* want to see the "full orbit" here.) Click Iterate.

25. Try increasing or decreasing the iteration depth of *both* iterations (the curve and the interiors) simultaneously. To do this, select everything and use the + and − keys as in step 19.

26. Hide points *C, D,* and *E.*

The Koch Snowflake

From here it's not too hard to construct the beautiful figure known as the Koch snowflake. First you'll create a new custom tool to repeat everything you've done so far. Then you'll construct an equilateral triangle and apply your new custom tool to its other two sides.

27. Select everything in the sketch by choosing **Select All** from the Edit menu.

28. Choose **Create New Tool** from the Custom Tools menu in the Toolbox. Enter the name Snowflake Edge and click OK.

You may need to scroll down or increase the size of your sketch window to see the rotated point.

29. Rotate point A by 60° around point B. To do this, double-click point B to mark it as a center. Then select point A and choose **Rotate** from the Transform menu. The value for Angle should already be set to 60, so click Rotate.

30. Construct the triangle interior defined by the three points in your sketch.

    See step 22 if you need a reminder how to do this.

What would happen if you clicked on points in the order opposite to that described in step 31? Try it and see.

31. Apply the **Snowflake Edge** tool to the other two sides of the new interior. To do this, choose **Snowflake Edge** from the Custom Tools menu. Click on B and A' to make one side and then on A' and A to make the other.

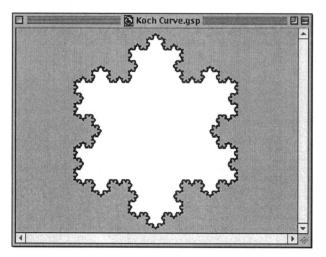

32. Hide all points in the sketch, save it (for posterity), then kick up your heels and relax—you've completed the introductory tours!

The Geometer's Sketchpad Learning Guide

Appendix: Quick Command Reference

This is a menu-by-menu listing of all of Sketchpad's commands with a brief description of each. See the Online Reference Manual (accessed through the Help menu) or the *Reference Manual* for more detailed information.

File Menu

New Sketch	Opens a new, blank document.
Open	Opens one or more previously saved documents.
Save	Saves changes made to the active document since the last time it was saved.
Save As	Names and saves the active document in a location that you specify.
Close	Closes the current document window.
Document Options	Manages the pages and custom tools contained in a document.
Page Setup	Sets up the page size, orientation, and other printing options for your document.
Print Preview	Displays a preview of your document as it will appear when printed.
Print	Prints the current page of the active document.
Quit	Closes all open documents and exits Sketchpad.

Edit Menu

Undo	Undoes the most recently performed action.
Redo	Redoes an action you have previously undone.
Cut	Removes selected objects, along with any objects that depend on them. Objects are placed on the clipboard to be pasted into a sketch or another application.
Copy	Places a copy of selected objects on the clipboard to be pasted into a sketch or another application.
Paste	Pastes the contents of the clipboard into the active sketch.
Clear	Removes selected objects, along with any objects that depend on them.
Action Buttons	Creates one of several types of action buttons. (Action buttons are sketch objects that, when pressed, perform a previously defined action, such as starting an animation or hiding a group of objects.)
Select All	Selects all objects if a **Selection Arrow** or **Custom** tool is active, or all objects that match any other active tool.
Select Parents	Selects the parents of each selected object. (The *parents* of an object are those objects upon which the object directly depends.)
Select Children	Selects the children of each selected object. (The *children* of an object are those objects that directly depend on the object.)
Split/ Merge	Allows you to alter relationships among objects by splitting points from their parents, merging points with other points or onto paths, and by merging several text objects into one.
Edit Definition (Edit Calculation, Edit Function, Edit Parameter, or Edit Plotted Point)	Allows you to edit the definition of the selected calculation, function, numeric parameters, or plotted points.
Properties	Allows you to change a variety of properties of a single selected object.
Preferences	Allows you to change a variety of settings that determine how Sketchpad works.

Display Menu

Line Width	Sets the line width of each selected object to dashed, thin, or thick.
Color	Sets the color of each selected object.
Text	Sets the font used—or increases or decreases the font size—for the selected objects.
Hide Objects	Hides selected objects from view without changing their geometric role in the sketch.
Show All Hidden	Displays and selects all objects previously hidden in a sketch.
Show/ Hide Labels	Shows or hides the labels of selected objects.
Trace	Turns tracing on or off for selected objects.
Erase Traces	Removes all visible traces from the screen.
Animate	Puts each selected geometric object into motion.
Increase Speed	Increases or decreases the speed of selected animating objects (or of all animating objects if nothing is selected).
Decrease Speed	
Stop Animation/ Stop All Motions	Stops the motion of selected animating objects (or of all animating objects if nothing is selected).
Show/Hide Text Palette	Shows or hides the Text Palette.
Show/Hide Motion Controller	Shows or hides the Motion Controller.
Show/Hide Toolbox	Shows or hides Sketchpad's Toolbox.

Construct Menu

Point On Object	*Selection prerequisites: One or more path objects.* Constructs a point on each selected path object.
Midpoint	*Selection prerequisites: One or more segments.* Constructs a point at the midpoint of each selected segment.
Intersection	*Selection prerequisites: Two intersecting objects.* Constructs a point at each intersection of the two selected objects.
Segment **Ray** **Line**	*Selection prerequisites: Two or more points.* Constructs a segment, ray, or line through the selected points. (The **Ray** command constructs a ray from the first point through the second.) If more than two points are selected, constructs the same number of objects as the number of selected points.
Parallel Line	*Selection prerequisites: A straight object and one or more points; or a point and one or more straight objects.* Constructs a line through each selected point parallel to each selected straight object.
Perpendicular Line	*Selection prerequisites: A straight object and one or more points; or a point and one or more straight objects.* Constructs a line through each selected point perpendicular to each selected straight object.
Angle Bisector	*Selection prerequisites: Three points, with the vertex point selected second.* Constructs a ray that bisects the angle formed by the three selected points.
Circle By Center+Point	*Selection prerequisites: Two points.* Constructs a circle with its center at the first selected point and its circumference passing through the second selected point.

The Geometer's Sketchpad Learning Guide

Construct Menu (continued)

Circle By Center+Radius	*Selection prerequisites: A point and one or more segments and/or distance measurements; or a segment or distance measurement and one or more points.* Constructs one or more circles centered at each selected point and with the radius determined by each selected segment or distance measurement.
Arc On Circle	*Selection prerequisites: A circle and two points on that circle; or a center point and two other points equally distant from the center point.* Constructs an arc on the given circle or with the given center, bounded by the selected circumference points.
Arc Through 3 Points	*Selection prerequisites: Three noncollinear points; that is, three points that do not lie on the same line.* Constructs an arc through the three selected points. The arc starts at the first selected point, passes through the second, and ends at the third.
Interior **(Polygon Interior,** **Circle Interior,** **Arc Sector Interior, or** **Arc Segment Interior)**	*Selection prerequisites: Three or more points; one or more circles; or one or more arcs.* Constructs a polygon interior with the selected points as vertices, or a circle interior for each selected circle, or an arc sector or arc segment interior for each selected arc.
Locus	*Selection prerequisites: The object whose locus you wish to construct (the driven object) and a point (the driver) that determines the position of that object.* Constructs the locus of the selected object as the driver point moves along its path.

Transform Menu

Mark Center	Marks the most recently selected point as the center about which future rotations and dilations will occur.
Mark Mirror	Marks the most recently selected straight object as the mirror across which future reflections will occur.
Mark Angle	*Selection prerequisites: Three points or an angle measurement.* Marks the most recently selected angle or angle measurement as the angle to be used for future rotations and polar translations.
Mark Ratio/ Mark Segment Ratio/ Scale Factor	*Selection prerequisites: Three collinear points, two segments, or a unitless measurement.* Marks the most recently selected ratio or scale factor as the ratio for future dilations.
Mark Vector	Marks for future translations the vector determined by the two most recently selected points.
Mark Distance	Marks the one or two most recently selected distance measurement(s) for future polar and rectangular translations.
Translate	Constructs a translated image of the selected geometric object(s).
Rotate	Constructs a rotated image of the selected object(s).
Dilate	Constructs a dilated image of the selected object(s).
Reflect	Constructs a mirror image of the selected object(s) across a marked mirror.
Iterate	*Selection prerequisites: One or more independent (pre-image) points or parameters that define one or more dependent (image) points or calculations.* Constructs the iterated images of a set of related geometric objects according to an iteration rule that you define.

The Geometer's Sketchpad Learning Guide

Measure Menu

Length	*Selection prerequisites: One or more segments.*
	Measures the lengths of the selected segments.
Distance	*Selection prerequisites: Two points, or one point and one straight object.*
	Measures the distance between two points, or the distance from a point to a straight object.
Perimeter	*Selection prerequisites: One or more polygons, arc sectors, or arc segment interiors.*
	Measures the perimeter of each selected polygon or arc interior.
Circumference	*Selection prerequisites: One or more circles or circle interiors.*
	Measures the circumference of each selected circle or circle interior.
Angle	*Selection prerequisites: Three points.*
	Measures the angle defined by the three selected points (the second selected point is the vertex).
Area	*Selection prerequisites: One or more interiors or circles.*
	Measures the area of each selected polygon interior, circle, circle interior, arc segment interior, or arc sector interior
Arc Angle	*Selection prerequisites: One or more arcs, or a circle and two or three points on the circle.*
	Measures the angle of each selected arc.
Arc Length	*Selection prerequisites: One or more arcs, or a circle and two or three points on the circle.*
	Measures the length of each selected arc.
Radius	*Selection prerequisites: One or more circles, circle interiors, arcs, or arc interiors.*
	Measures the radius of each selected circle, circle interior, arc, arc sector interior, or arc segment interior.
Ratio	*Selection prerequisites: Two segments or three collinear points.*
	Measures the ratio of the lengths of the segments.

Measure Menu (continued)

Calculate	Opens Sketchpad's Calculator.
Coordinates	*Selection prerequisites: One or more points.* Measures the coordinates of each selected point with respect to the marked coordinate system.
Abscissa (x)	*Selection prerequisites: One or more points.* Measures the abscissa (x-value) of each selected point with respect to the marked coordinate system.
Ordinate (y)	*Selection prerequisites: One or more points.* Measures the ordinate (y-value) of each selected point with respect to the marked coordinate system.
Coordinate Distance	*Selection prerequisites: Two points.* Measures the distance between the two points based on the marked coordinate system.
Slope	*Selection prerequisites: One or more straight objects.* Measures the slope of each selected line with respect to the marked coordinate system.
Equation	*Selection prerequisites: One or more lines or circles.* Measures the equation of each selected object with respect to the marked coordinate system.

Graph Menu

Define Coordinate System/ **Define Origin/** **Define Unit Circle/** **Define Unit Distance/** **Define Unit Distances**	*Selection prerequisites: One point, one circle, one defining distance, one point and one defining distance, two defining distances, one point and two defining distances, or nothing. (A defining distance can be a segment or a distance measurement.)* Creates and marks a new coordinate system. The type and scale of the coordinate system depend on what is selected.
Mark Coordinate System	*Selection prerequisites: A coordinate system's axis, origin point, unit point, unit circle, or grid.* Marks the coordinate system associated with the selected object as the coordinate system on which to measure or plot new objects.
Grid Form	Changes the grid appearance and scaling of the marked coordinate system. Choices are square, rectangular, and polar.
Show/Hide Grid	Shows or hides the grid lines of the marked coordinate system.
Snap Points	Turns on or off point snapping, which causes independent points to snap to nearby locations when you create or drag them.
Plot Points/ **Plot As (x, y)/** **Plot As (r, theta)/** **Plot Table Data**	With nothing selected, plots one or more points on the marked coordinate system. With two measurements selected, plots a point at the coordinates given by those measurements' values. With a single table selected, plots points at coordinates given by that table's data. In all cases, the Grid Form setting determines whether coordinate pairs are plotted as (x, y) or $(r, theta)$.
New Parameter	Creates a new parameter. (A parameter is a number that can easily be changed.)
New Function	Opens the function calculator and allows you to create a new function.
Plot Function/ **Plot New Function**	Plots one or more selected functions, or creates and plots a new function if no objects are selected.

Derivative	Creates a new function that is the derivative of the selected function with respect to that function's independent variable.
Tabulate	Creates a table of values for the selected measurement(s).
Add Table Data	Adds a row to the selected table, or starts automatic data collection for the selected table.
Remove Table Data	Deletes the last row or all rows from the selected table.

Window Menu (Microsoft Windows and Macintosh OS X only)

The Window menu presents a list of all open documents and gives options for arranging document windows.

Help Menu

Choosing any command in the Help menu launches your web browser and opens Sketchpad's help system to the appropriate page.